How to Clean:

Daily, Weekly, and Monthly Strategies for a Cleaner, Healthier Home

By Christine Carter

Contents

Introduction

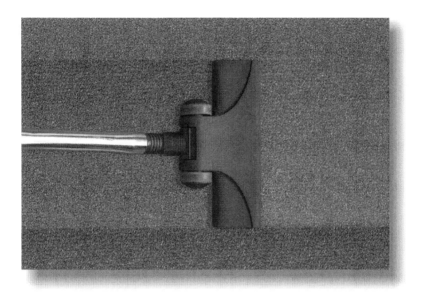

At its core, cleaning is simply the process of removing dirt from the home. 'Dirt' can refer to everything from the dust that gathers on the bookshelves, to the soap scum in the tub, to that persistent mold or mildew that crops up in the tile grout. Luckily, keeping the home clean doesn't have to take hours out of your busy week! With the right strategies in your cleaning toolbox, it's entirely possible to keep your home clean and healthy without expending unmanageable amounts of time or energy. The purpose of this book is to help you fill your cleaning toolbox with strategies, tips, and ticks to save you time and take the headaches out of housework.

The Importance of Cleaning

Like it or not, our homes are subject to deterioration. Dirt, grime and the germs that can accompany them will continue to build up unless we take the time to clean. Without intervention, homes can become unsightly at best and unsafe at worst. Some of the most important reasons to clean house are health, manageability, and comfort.

Health: Dust, mold, and mildew can contribute to allergies and breathing problems, while the bacteria that can crop up in kitchens, bathrooms, and other areas can cause illness. Keeping allergens and bacteria under control is important for a safe, healthy living space.

Manageability: The plain truth is that homes take upkeep. That upkeep will be much more manageable with regular cleaning strategies in place. Put simply, it's much easier to clean a toilet that has been wiped down every week than one that hasn't been touched in six months! A simple in investment in quick daily and weekly cleaning rituals will keep the overall cleaning maintenance of your home at a manageable level, so that you don't get backed up or overwhelmed.

Comfort: Clean homes usually lead to more relaxing, comfortable living spaces. A clean home smells fresher, is easier to breathe in thanks to less dust and allergens, and looks both brighter and more put together. Further, cleaning supports both organizing and decluttering, which make it easier to find things in the home and manage our belongings (check out my books on decluttering and organizing for specific tips and strategies).

Green Cleaning

Green strategies and green alternatives have been included throughout this book to help you avoid harsh chemicals that may be bad for your health, your household items, and the environment. Most of the green cleaning recipes in this book rely on low-cost, natural ingredients that you can obtain from your local supermarket and are simple to prepare and store.

What This Book Will Cover

This book will start with a look at basic principles for simple, fast cleaning. These principles can be applied to every room in the house and will support your cleaning efforts from daily maintenance to spring cleaning. Once these basic principles have been discussed, we'll move on to creating a cleaning plan for daily, weekly, and monthly upkeep, including some handy checklists to help you streamline the process. After this, we'll step into a room by room look at specific cleaning strategies with a focus on saving you time and energy. Finally, we've compiled an appendix of green cleaning recipes that you can use to help keep your rituals environmentally friendly and safe.

1. Basic Principles for Fast and Easy Cleaning

Five basic principles underlie the strategies in this book. These principles will help ensure that house cleaning is quick, simple, and effective.

Principle #1: Categorize Tasks by Frequency

Not all cleaning tasks need to be done every day – or even every week. Knowing whether a cleaning task needs to be done daily, weekly, or monthly can help you avoid wasting time cleaning things that don't need it and conversely, can help you avoid spending extra time and energy on grime that has built up because it wasn't kept up.

Principle #2: Don't Underestimate the Power of Upkeep

Small upkeep tasks - like wiping down the stovetop after you cook – can be the first to go when life gets busy because they don't *seem* that important. After all, what's the big deal if the stove doesn't get wiped down after dinner for a few days? However, these small daily and weekly tasks – many of which take under 60 seconds to complete – will make weekly and monthly cleaning much more manageable and much less time consuming. When it comes to keeping up with keeping up, there are two basic approaches:

1. *Do upkeep tasks in chunks.* With this approach, you set aside chunks of time for upkeep. For example, you might decide to do all the dishes from the day at night, in one fell swoop, or to spend 20-30 minutes at the end of the day doing all of your upkeep tasks at once.
2. *Plan your tasks around your life.* This is the keep-up-as-you-go approach. For example, as opposed to doing all the dishes at the end of the day, you rinse them and put them in the dishwasher immediately after use. With this approach, you take care of small upkeep tasks throughout the day, whenever it makes the most sense to do so.

Pro tip: These two approaches don't just apply to daily upkeep; you can divide weekly and monthly, and yearly tasks this way, too! Would you rather do all of your monthly cleaning chores in one hardcore weekend? Or would you rather divide them up with your weekly tasks so that you never have to spend too much time cleaning on any given Saturday?

In this book, we will focus primarily on the second approach as many people find it more manageable to spend a couple of minutes here and there on upkeep tasks than to carve out bigger chunks of time, especially at the end of a long day. However, if you prefer the chunking method, go for it! The strategies presented in this book, by and large, will work well either way. The key is to find which approach fits best for *you*.

Principle #3: Keep Cleaning Products Accessible

This is especially true for those small daily and weekly cleaning tasks, and integral to the idea of planning your tasks around your life. If you keep a spray bottle of all-purpose cleaner under the bathroom sink, it's no big deal to give the counter top a wipe-down twice a week after you shower. When we have to go looking for cleaning products and carry them off to be put back after use, we are less likely to take the time to do upkeep. Just make sure that wherever your cleaning products are kept, they are stored safely and are inaccessible to small children and pets.

Principle #4: Don't Be Afraid to Do Less

In spite of our best efforts, sometimes there simply will not be time to accomplish all of our cleaning tasks in a given day or week, even the small ones. When this happens, it can be easy to feel overwhelmed and either avoid or actively give up doing any cleaning at all. However, even minimal upkeep is always better than none! Remember, those tiny tasks during the week are what make the monthly tasks a snap. The watchword of Principle #4 is *prioritize* - if all you have is 5 minutes at the end of the day, use them wisely and don't stress about the rest. While those 5 minutes may feel incomplete, they will lessen the load on your weekly and monthly cleaning sessions and help slow down the pileup.

Principle #5: Clean Green

The importance of using natural, environmentally friendly cleaning products whenever possible can't be stressed enough. Avoid using harsh chemicals whenever you can. Instead, choose cleaning products that are good for the environment, you, and your family. Be smart with recycling and reusing. Armed with knowledge and forethought, you can make your home greener, cleaner, and healthier!

3. Cleaning the Kitchen

Part I: Cleaning Tips and Strategies for the Kitchen

Sink

Daily:

- Spray down the sink and faucet with all-purpose cleaner (see chapter 10 for all-purpose cleaner recipes), wipe, and rinse. This can be done quickly and easily right after you finish up the dishes. Rinse out the dishrag and use it to wipe down the sink, then rinse again.

- Wipe down the backsplash behind the sink and any tile or laminate between the back of the sink and the wall.

Weekly:

- Scrub the sink and faucet with baking soda. Spray down with white or cleaning vinegar. Rinse with warm water.
- Scrub the backsplash behind the sink and any tile or laminate between the back of the sink and the wall.

Monthly:

- Clean out the disposal. *Method 1:* Run ice cubes made of 50% water, 50% vinegar (or 50% water, 50% lemon juice) through the disposal. *Method 2:* Run cold water through the disposal for 30 seconds. Shut off the water and the disposal and add ¼ - ½ cup baking soda. Let sit for 5 minutes. Add a cup of vinegar. Run cold water through the disposal for 10-20 seconds.
- Use the *Grout Cleaner* recipe in chapter 10 to clean the grout.

Stove and Vent

Daily:

- Wipe down the stove, including the surface and knobs.

Weekly:

- Wash the stove top, including the grooves and display. Tip: An old pen (or mechanical pencil with no lead if you prefer) pressed into a wet rag makes a handy tool for scraping grime out of narrow grooves around the edge of the stove.

- Wash the stove drip pans and gas grates by soaking them in warm soapy water and then scrubbing or running them through the dishwasher. For stubborn grease, apply a past made of 2 parts baking soda and 1 part water and let it sit for 60 min; scrub and rinse. If you have a gas stove with removable elements, wash them as well.
- Wipe down the vent hood.

Monthly:

- Degrease the vent hood. Here is a perfect example of how upkeep can make your life easier in the long run. Scrubbing grease from a neglected vent hood frustrating and time-consuming. Make life easier by degreasing the vent hood every month. Combined with your weekly wipe-down, this will keep your vent good shiny and easy to deal with when you do your annual deep cleaning. See chapter 10 for a natural degreaser recipe.

Oven

Daily:

- Wipe down the front of the oven and the door handle with all-purpose cleaner.

Weekly:

- Wipe down or vacuum out the inside of the oven.

Monthly:

- Clean the oven. Begin by removing oven racks and vacuuming or wiping out any crumbs or debris that may have fallen to the oven floor. Next, mix ¾ cup baking soda with 3-4 Tablespoons of water to create a paste. Using cleaning gloves, spread the paste over the walls, back, and floor of the oven, being careful not to get it on any of the heating elements or convection fan. Rub the mixture in as you spread. Leave it to sit overnight, then take a damp sponge or rag and wipe up any loose paste. Spray with vinegar and warm water; allow the remaining baking soda to foam. Let sit for 5-10 more minutes, then wipe up with a wet rag. Continue to wipe clean with vinegar spray and a wet rag until the oven is clean.

Counters

Daily:

- Put away any items that have been left out on the counters.
- Wipe down the counters with all-purpose cleaner.

Weekly:

- Do a deeper wipe-down, making sure to get the corners and any joints or seams where food may become stuck.
- Pull out counter-top appliances and containers and wipe down the counter underneath them.
- Take care of any countertop stains. Check out the *Countertop Stain-Remover and Disinfectant* in chapter 10 for a natural stain remover.

Monthly:

- None.

Refrigerator

Daily:

- Wipe down the outside of the refrigerator.

Weekly:

- Dust the top of the refrigerator
- Disinfect the handles
- Throw out any expired food
- Wipe down the shelves and drawers.

Monthly:

- Deep clean the refrigerator. Remove all food products, drawers, and shelves. Spray down walls, floor, ceiling, and built-in storage with hydrogen peroxide and water, then wipe up with a damp cloth. Wash removable drawers and shelves with soap and warm water then dry with a microfiber cloth before returning them to the refrigerator. Return food products. Clean the outside of the refrigerator, including the top, with all-purpose cleaner.

Microwave

Daily:

- Wipe down the front of the microwave

Weekly:

- Wipe down the outside of the microwave
- Wash the glass plate by hand or in the dishwasher if allowed
- Wash the inside of the microwave. If food or spills are stuck to the walls and sides, try microwaving a bowl of water for 2 minutes; the steam will loosen the grime so it's easier to wipe out. You can also add wedges of lemon or orange or a couple tablespoons of vinegar to the water to help get rid of odors.

Monthly:

- Nothing! If you've been taking care of daily and weekly upkeep, there should be nothing left to do at the monthly level.

Appliances

Daily:

- Wipe up any splatters or spills that may have gotten to your appliances. This is best done when the splatter or spill happens, but can also easily be done at the same time you wipe down the counter.

Weekly:

- Wipe down the faces of all appliances sitting on the counter. This can easily be done at the same time that you wipe down the counter.

Monthly:

- Pull out all appliances sitting on the counter and wipe them down, including cords (make sure cords are unplugged).

Cupboards and Drawers

Daily:

- Wipe down the outsides of the cupboards and drawers.

Weekly:

- Wipe down the insides of cupboard doors, particularly those that get opened closed a lot – you might be surprised by just how quickly sticky fingers can make a mess of the inside of a cupboard door!

Monthly:

- Wipe out high- and medium-use cupboards and drawers, such as the utensil drawer and everyday dish cupboards.
- Dust the tops of kitchen cupboards. Dust the bottom of hanging cupboards.

Floor

Daily:

- Sweep the floor.
- Use a damp microfiber cloth or rag to wipe up any spills or noticeable spots.

Weekly:

- Mop the floor. Use soap and water to mop laminate floors. For tile floors, combine 1 cup of baking soda with 2 gallons of water in your mop bucket. For wood floors, use the *Wood Floor Cleaner* recipe in chapter 10.
- Wipe down the baseboards.
- Clean off all scuff marks.

Monthly:

- No monthly tasks.

Walls and Doors

Daily:

- Wipe up any splatters that may have happened during the day (especially around the stove); otherwise, let them be!

Weekly:

- Wipe down door handles, and door frames. Don't forget to check around the door handle – this is prime fingerprint territory.
- Wipe down the walls in high-use areas, such as the wall behind the stove and the wall behind the sink.
- Wipe down light switches and outlets.
- Clean off any scuff marks that have accumulated.

Monthly:

- Wash the walls with a mild solution of soap and water (3-4 drops of liquid castile soap to 1 gallon of warm water) or mix vinegar and warm water (2-3 Tablespoons of distilled white vinegar to 1 gallon of warm water). Don't soak the walls – instead, wet a soft sponge in the cleaning solution, wring it out, and gently wash the walls. Make sure that the sponge is nearly dry before washing around outlets and light switches. Disconnect power to outlets for an added safety measure.
Trash Cans

Daily:

- Take out the trash and recycling if they are full or smell.

Weekly:

- Take out the trash and recycling at least weekly, regardless of whether they are full.
- Wipe down the front/lid of the trashcan and recycling containers.

Monthly:

- Wash out the trashcans and recycling containers. It's often easiest to take them into the yard, spray them down with all-purpose cleaning spray, then spray them out with the hose. Wipe them down with a cleaning rag to get rid of any remaining residue, then turn them upside down to air dry.

Part II: Kitchen Checklists

DAILY KITCHEN CHECKLIST

Tip: Rather than viewing the following tasks as separate, save time by combining them. For example, move in a smooth sweep through the kitchen, wiping down the various surfaces as you go.

	TASKS
☐	Spray down the sink and faucet with all-purpose cleaner, wipe, and rinse.
☐	Wipe down the backsplash behind the sink and any tile or laminate between the back of the sink and the wall.
☐	Wipe down the stove, including the surface and knobs.
☐	Wipe down the front of the oven and the over door handle.
☐	Put away any items that have been left out on the counters.

☐	Wipe down the counters with a mild disinfectant.
☐	Wipe down the outside of the refrigerator.
☐	Wipe down the front of the microwave
☐	Wipe up any splatters or spills that may have gotten to appliances.
☐	Wipe down the outsides of the cupboards and drawers.
☐	Sweep the floor.
☐	Use a damp cloth or rag to wipe up any spills or noticeable spots.
☐	Wipe up any splatters that may have happened during the day.
☐	Take out the trash and recycling if they are full or smell.

WEEKLY KITCHEN CHECKLIST

	TASKS
☐	Scrub the sink and faucet.
☐	Scrub the backsplash behind the sink and any tile or laminate between the back of the sink and the wall.
☐	Wash the stove top.
☐	Wash the stove drip pans or gas grates.
☐	Wipe down the vent hood.
☐	Wipe down or vacuum out the inside of the oven.
☐	Wash the counters.
☐	Pull out counter-top appliances and containers and wipe down the counter underneath them.
☐	Remove any countertop stains.
☐	Dust the top of the refrigerator.
☐	Disinfect the refrigerator door handles.
☐	Throw out any expired food.
☐	Wipe down the shelves and drawers.
☐	Wipe down the outside of the microwave
☐	Wash the microwave's glass plate.
☐	Wash the inside of the microwave.
☐	Wipe down the faces of all appliances sitting on the

	counter.
☐	Wipe down the insides of cupboard doors.
☐	Mop the floor.
☐	Wipe down the baseboards.
☐	Clean off all scuff marks.
☐	Wipe down door handles, and door frames.
☐	Wipe down the walls in high-use areas.
☐	Wipe down light switches and outlets.
☐	Clean off any scuff marks that have accumulated.
☐	Take out the trash and recycling at least weekly, regardless of whether they are full.
☐	Wipe down the front/lid of the trashcan and recycling containers.

MONTHLY KITCHEN CHECKLIST

	TASKS
☐	Clean out the disposal.
☐	Clean the grout.
☐	Degrease the vent hood.
☐	Clean the oven.
☐	Deep clean the refrigerator.
☐	Pull out all appliances sitting on the counter and wipe them down, including cords (make sure cords are unplugged).
☐	Wipe out high- and medium-use cupboards and drawers.
☐	Dust the tops of kitchen cupboards.
☐	Dust the bottom of hanging cupboards.
☐	Wash the walls.
☐	Wash out the trashcans and recycling containers.

4. Cleaning the Living Room

Part I: Cleaning Tips and Strategies for the Living Room

Walls

Daily:

- Wipe down any visible splatters from the day with a wet rag or all-purpose cleaner, otherwise, let them be.

Weekly:

- Wipe down the walls.
- Wipe down the light switches and outlets.

- Clean up any scuffmarks that have accumulated during the week. For stubborn scuff marks, use castile soap and warm water.

Monthly:

- Wash the walls with a mild solution of soap and water (3-4 drops of liquid castile soap to 1 gallon of warm water) or mix vinegar and warm water (2-3 Tablespoons of distilled white vinegar to 1 gallon of warm water). Don't soak the walls – instead, wet a soft sponge in the cleaning solution, wring it out, and gently wash the walls. Make sure that the sponge is nearly dry before washing around outlets and light switches. Disconnect power to outlets for an added safety measure.

Tables

Daily:

- Straighten magazines and put away anything that has been left out on a table

Weekly:

- Wipe down the coffee table and any other high-use tables such as catch-alls and end tables.

Monthly:

- Use all-purpose cleaner to wipe out any drawers and cupboards built into your tables.

Upholstered Furniture

Daily:

- Straighten cushions.
- Fold throws.

Weekly:

- Clean out items that may have fallen between or under seat cushions.
- Vacuum the furniture.

Monthly:

- Clean under and behind furniture in preparation for vacuuming the floor.

Book Shelves

Daily:

- Straighten books and other items.

Weekly:

- Dust the exposed surfaces of the shelves and the tops of the shelves.

Monthly:

- Clean up items that have fallen under or behind bookshelves in preparation for vacuuming.

Light Fixtures

Daily:

- Unless something has spilled or splattered on them, let them be.

- Dust all light fixtures, including table lamps, standing lamps, ceiling fixtures, and ceiling fans.

Monthly:

- Wipe down all light fixtures. Avoid wiping the bulbs and make sure they are cool and turned off before you begin.

Floors

Daily:

- Walk through and pick up anything that has been left out on the floor, such as toys, clothes, or bags.

Weekly:

- Vacuum or shake out area rugs.
- Vacuum the carpet or sweep and mop the floor. For wood floors, use the *Wood Floor Cleaner* recipe in chapter 10. For laminate floors, a simple solution of warm water and castile soap will do the trick. For tile floors, combine 1 cup of baking soda with 2 gallons of water in your mop bucket.
- Wipe down all baseboards.
- Clean up any scuff marks.

Monthly:

- Vacuum or sweep and mop under and behind all furniture.

Windows/Window Treatments

Daily:

- Open and close curtains/blinds at the appropriate times of day.

Weekly:

- Wipe down blinds.
- Wipe down windows.
- Dust off the tops of all window treatments.

Monthly:

- None

Part II: Living Room Checklists

DAILY LIVING ROOM CHECKLIST

	TASK
☐	Wipe down any visible splatters on the wall.
☐	Straighten magazines and put away anything that has been left out on a table
☐	Straighten cushions.
☐	Fold throws.
☐	Straighten books and other items on the bookshelves.
☐	Walk through and pick up anything that has been left out on the floor, such as toys, clothes, or bags.
☐	Open and close curtains/blinds at the appropriate times of day.

WEEKLY LIVING ROOM CHECKLIST

	TASKS
☐	Wipe down the walls.
☐	Wipe down the light switches and outlets.
☐	Clean up any scuffmarks that have accumulated during the week.
☐	Wipe down the coffee table and any other high-use tables such as catch-alls and end tables.
☐	Clean out items that may have fallen between or under seat cushions.
☐	Vacuum the furniture.
☐	Dust the exposed surfaces of the shelves and the tops of the shelves.
☐	Dust all light fixtures, including table lamps, standing lamps, ceiling fixtures, and ceiling fans.
☐	Vacuum or shake out area rugs.
☐	Vacuum the carpet or sweep and mop the floor.

☐	Wipe down all baseboards.
☐	Clean up any scuff marks.
☐	Wipe down blinds.
☐	Wipe down windows.
☐	Dust off the tops of all window treatments.

MONTHLY LIVING ROOM CHECKLIST

	TASKS
☐	Wash the walls.
☐	Wipe out any drawers and cupboards built into your tables.
☐	Clean under and behind furniture.
☐	Clean up items that have fallen under or behind.
☐	Wipe down all light fixtures.
☐	Vacuum or sweep and mop under and behind all furniture.

5. Cleaning the Dining Room

Part I: Cleaning Tips and Strategies for the Dining Room

China Hutch

Daily:

- Put away any items that may have gathered on the hutch.

Weekly:

- Dust the front and sides of the china hutch.

Monthly:

- Wash any glass display fronts or 'windows' on the cupboards.
- Wipe out the shelves.
- Dust the top of the china hutch.

Table

Daily:

- Wipe down the table after use. If you are using a table cloth, wipe off any crumbs or shake out. Replace if anything wet or sticky has spilled on the table cloth.
- Brush any crumbs from chairs and wipe down any sticky spots.

Weekly:

- Wipe down chairs with all-purpose cleaner.

Monthly:

- Wipe down the legs and braces of the table with all-purpose cleaner.

Floors

Daily:

- Sweep, especially under the table and chairs.
- Spot-mop any spills or drips with a wet rag.

Weekly:

- Sweep and mop or vacuum the floor.
- Wipe down all baseboards.
- Clean off any scuffmarks.
- Wipe off light switches and outlet covers.

Monthly:

- Sweep and mop or vacuum behind and under all furniture.

Window Treatments

Daily:

- Open and close blinds and curtains as appropriate.

Weekly:

- Wipe down blinds and windows.
- Wipe out the window tracks.

Monthly:

- Wash the inside window panes.
- Wash the outside window panes quarterly.

Doors and Walls

Daily:

- Wipe down any spills or splatters that occurred during the day.

Weekly:

- Wipe down the walls.
- Wipe down the doorframes and door handles.
- Wipe down outlet covers and light switches.

Monthly:

- Wash the walls and doors with a mild solution of soap and water (3-4 drops of liquid castile soap to 1 gallon of warm water) or mix vinegar and warm water (2-3 Tablespoons of distilled white vinegar to 1 gallon of warm water). Don't soak the walls –

instead, wet a soft sponge in the cleaning solution, wring it out, and gently wash the walls. Make sure that the sponge is nearly dry before washing around outlets and light switches. Disconnect power to outlets for an added safety measure.

Light Fixtures

Daily:

- No daily tasks.

Weekly:

- Dust all light fixtures.

Monthly:

- Wipe down all light fixtures. Avoid wiping the bulbs and make sure they are cool and turned off before you begin.

Part II: Dining Room Checklists

DAILY DINING ROOM CHECKLIST

	TASKS
☐	Put away any items that may have gathered on the china hutch.
☐	Wipe down the table after use. If you are using a table cloth, wipe off any crumbs or shake out. Replace if anything wet or sticky has spilled on the table cloth.
☐	Brush any crumbs from chairs and wipe down any sticky spots.
☐	Sweep, especially under the table and chairs.
☐	Spot-mop any spills or drips with a wet rag.
☐	Open and close blinds and curtains as appropriate.
☐	Wipe down any spills or splatters on doors and walls that occurred during the day.

WEEKLY DINING ROOM CHECKLIST

	TASKS
☐	Dust the front and sides of the china hutch.
☐	Wipe down chairs with all-purpose cleaner.
☐	Sweep and mop or vacuum the floor.
☐	Wipe down all baseboards.
☐	Clean off any scuffmarks.
☐	Wipe off light switches and outlet covers.
☐	Wipe down blinds and windows.
☐	Wipe out the window tracks.
☐	Wipe down the walls.
☐	Wipe down the doorframes and door handles.
☐	Dust all light fixtures.

MONTHLY DINING ROOM CHECKLIST

	TASKS
☐	Wash any glass display fronts or 'windows' on the china hutch.
☐	Wipe out the shelves of the china hutch.
☐	Dust the top of the china hutch.
☐	Wipe down the legs and braces of the table with all-purpose cleaner.
☐	Sweep and mop or vacuum behind and under all furniture.
☐	Wash the inside window panes.
☐	Wash the outside window panes quarterly.
☐	Wash the walls and doors.
☐	Wipe down all light fixtures. Avoid wiping the bulbs and make sure they are cool and turned off before you begin.

6. Cleaning the Bathrooms

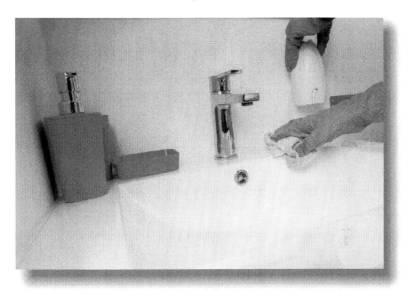

Part I: Cleaning Tips and Strategies for the Bathrooms

Floors

Daily:

- Sweep the floors.

Weekly:

- Mop the floors. For wood floors, use the *Wood Floor Cleaner* recipe in chapter 10. For laminate floors, a simple solution of warm water and castile soap will do the trick.
- Wipe down the baseboards.
- Clean up all scuff marks.
- Wash bathroom mats and rugs.

Monthly:

- If you have tile floors, use the *Grout Cleaner* recipe in chapter 10 to clean the grout.

Tub/Shower

Daily:

- Spray the entire tub/shower, including walls, floor, faucets, and showerhead, with vinegar and water. No need to rinse.
- Wipe any hair off of the drain.

Weekly:

- Scrub the tub/shower.

Monthly:

- Clean out the drain.
- Wash the shower curtain.
- Wash the shower mat.
- Remove mineral buildup from the shower head, as needed. Fill a plastic storage bag with 1-2 cups vinegar. Attach the bag to the showerhead so that the showerhead is resting in the vinegar. Let sit overnight, then remove the bag and wipe the shower head clean with warm water.
- Use the *Grout Cleaner* recipe in chapter 10 to clean the grout.

Toilet

Daily:

- Wipe down the seat and behind the seat. QuickTip: This can be done right after using the toilet, while you're already in the bathroom, at whatever point during the day you have an extra 30 seconds.

Weekly:

- Clean the outside of the toilet with all-purpose cleaner.
- Clean the toilet bowl. If your toilet bowl is in good condition, all purpose cleaner, allowed to sit for 15-20 minutes, should be sufficient to keep the john shining. For stubborn stains and mineral buildup, spray with vinegar and let sit for 10 minutes, then add 4 Tablespoons of baking soda, scrub, and flush.

Monthly:

- Clean the pipe behind the toilet.

Sink

Daily:

- Wipe down the sink and faucets, making sure to get rid of any old toothpaste that didn't get rinsed away.

Weekly:

- Add 4 Tbsp distilled white vinegar to a damp sponge and use it to wipe down the sink, counters, and faucets. No need to rinse.
- Use the *Grout Cleaner* recipe in chapter 10 to clean the grout and around the edges of the faucet.

Monthly:

- Clean the drain. Remove the plug and place it in a cup of distilled white vinegar. Run cold water for 5 minutes, then shut off the faucet. Pour 1 cup of distilled white vinegar down the drain. Wait 5 minutes, then pour 2 Tablespoons of baking powder down the drain. Wait 5 minutes more. Remove the plug from the vinegar and pour the vinegar down the drain. Wipe the plug clean and replace.

Counters

Daily:

- Put away anything that has been left out on a counter.
- Wipe down the counters.

Weekly:

- Wash the counters with distilled white vinegar, including between, under, and around any counter-top items such as toothbrush caddies or makeup boxes.
- Dust any items that reside on the counter.

Monthly:

- Run toothpaste holders and soap dispensers through the dishwasher or clean them with warm water and dish soap.

Mirrors

Daily:

- None.

Weekly:

- Clean the mirrors with vinegar-based all-purpose cleaner or glass cleaner (see chapter 10). Tip: Wash mirrors using old newspapers rather than rags or paper towels to get a truly streak-free shine.

Monthly:

- None.

Light Fixtures

Daily:

- No daily tasks.

Weekly:

- Dust all light fixtures.

Monthly:

- Wipe down all light fixtures. Avoid wiping the bulbs and make sure they are cool and turned off before you begin.

Window Treatments

Daily:

- Open and close blinds and curtains as appropriate.

Weekly:

- Wipe down the windows and blinds.
- Wipe out the window tracks.

Monthly:

- Clean the inside window panes.
- Wash curtains and blinds.
- Dust the top of the window treatment.

Cupboards, Drawers, and Shelving Units

Daily:

- Wipe down the fronts of cupboards, drawers and shelving units.

Weekly:

- Organize and straighten cupboards, drawers, and shelving units.
- Dust the top of cupboards and shelving units.

Monthly:

- Wipe out the insides of cupboards, drawers, and shelving units.

Doors and Walls

Daily:

- Wipe down any areas that have been splattered with bathroom products or that are prone to mildew.

Weekly:

- Wipe down walls, baseboards, and doorframes with all-purpose cleaner.
- Wipe down light switches and outlet covers.
- Wipe down door handles.
- Clean up any scuff marks.

Monthly:

- Wash the walls with a mild solution of soap and water (3-4 drops of liquid castile soap to 1 gallon of warm water) or mix vinegar and warm water (2-3 Tablespoons of distilled white vinegar to 1 gallon of warm water). Don't soak the walls – instead, wet a soft sponge in the cleaning solution, wring it out, and gently wash the walls. Make sure that the sponge is nearly dry before washing around outlets and light switches. Disconnect power to outlets for an added safety measure.

Ceiling

Daily:

- If you live in an area that is conducive to mildew, make sure to vent the bathroom during and after showers and baths, either by running the fan or cracking the window.

Weekly:

- Wipe down any areas that are prone to mildew.

Monthly:

- None.

Part II: Bathroom Checklists

DAILY BATHROOM CHECKLIST

	TABLE
☐	Sweep the floors.
☐	Wipe any hair off of the drain.
☐	Spray the entire tub/shower, including walls, floor, faucets, and showerhead, with vinegar and water. No need to rinse.
☐	Wipe down the seat and behind the seat.
☐	Wipe down the sink and faucets.
☐	Put away anything that has been left out on a counter.
☐	Wipe down the counters.
☐	Open and close blinds and curtains as appropriate.
☐	Wipe down the fronts of cupboards, drawers and shelving units.

☐	Wipe down any areas that have been splattered with bathroom products or that are prone to mildew.
☐	If you live in an area that is conducive to mildew, make sure to vent the bathroom during and after showers and baths, either by running the fan or cracking the window.

WEEKLY BATHROOM CHECKLIST

	TASK
☐	Mop the floors.
☐	Wipe down the baseboards.
☐	Clean up all scuff marks.
☐	Wash bathroom mats and rugs.
☐	Scrub the tub/shower.
☐	Clean the outside of the toilet with all-purpose cleaner.
☐	Clean the toilet bowl.
☐	Add 4 Tbsp distilled white vinegar to a damp sponge and use it to wipe down the sink, counters, and faucets. No need to rinse.
☐	Clean the grout.
☐	Wash between, under, and around any counter-top items such as toothbrush caddies or makeup boxes.
☐	Dust any items that reside on the counter.
☐	Clean the mirrors with vinegar-based all-purpose cleaner.
☐	Dust all light fixtures.
☐	Wipe down the windows and blinds.

☐	Wipe out the window tracks.
☐	Organize and straighten cupboards, drawers, and shelving units.
☐	Dust the top of cupboards and shelving units.
☐	Wash walls, baseboards, and doorframes.
☐	Wipe down light switches and outlet covers.
☐	Wipe down door handles.
☐	Clean up any scuff marks.
☐	Wipe down any areas of the ceiling that are prone to mildew.

MONTHLY BATHROOM CHECKLIST

	TASKS
☐	If you have tile floors, clean the grout.
☐	Clean out the drain.
☐	Wash the shower curtain.
☐	Wash the shower mat.
☐	Remove mineral buildup from the shower head, as needed.
☐	Clean the pipe behind the toilet.
☐	Clean the drain.
☐	Run toothpaste holders and soap dispensers through the dishwasher, or clean them with warm water and dish soap.
☐	Wipe down all light fixtures. Avoid wiping the bulbs and make sure they are cool and turned off before you begin.
☐	Clean the inside window panes.

☐	Wash curtains and blinds.
☐	Dust the top of the window treatment.
☐	Spray down the shower curtain with all purpose cleaner, vinegar based. Let sit for 10 minutes, then rinse with warm water.

7. Cleaning the Bedrooms

Part I: Cleaning Tips and Strategies for the Bedrooms

Floors

Daily:

- Pick up any toys, clothes, trash, or other items that have made their way to the floor during the day.

Weekly:

- Vacuum or mop the floor, as appropriate.
- Shake out area rugs.
- Wipe down all baseboards.
- Clean up any scuffmarks.

Monthly:

- Wash rugs. Note: castile soap can also be used to make laundry detergent!

Shelves

Daily:

- Straighten items on shelves and put away anything that doesn't belong there.

Weekly:

- Dust shelves, top and bottom.

Monthly:

- Wipe out shelves with all-purpose cleaner.

Beds

Daily:

- Make the bed and straighten the pillows.

Weekly:

- Dust the bedframe.
- Put away any items that have accumulated under the bed.
- Change the linens.

Monthly:

- Wipe down the bedframe with all-purpose cleaner.
- Wash the blankets.

Window Treatments

Daily:

- Open and close blinds and curtains as appropriate.

Weekly:

- Wipe down windows and blinds.
- Wipe out the window tracks.

Monthly:

- Wash the inside window panes.
- Wash the outside window panes quarterly.

Dressers

Daily:

- Straighten the top of the dresser and put away any clutter.

Weekly:

- Wipe down the dresser.
- Organize dresser drawers.

Monthly:

- Pick up and put away anything that has fallen behind or under the dresser in preparation for vacuuming/mopping.

Laundry

Daily:

- Place all dirty clothes in a hamper. For easy division of laundry come laundry day, try using a partitioned hamper or a separate hamper for colors, lights, and whites.

Weekly:

- Do the laundry. Even if it's a small batch, it's better to do laundry at least weekly to keep odors from gathering for too long.
- Put away laundry as soon as possible, to reduce both wrinkles and the likelihood that it will be forgotten or avoided.

Monthly:

- No monthly tasks (see '**Beds**')

Light Fixtures

Daily:

- No daily tasks.

Weekly:

- Dust all light fixtures.

Monthly:

- Wipe down all light fixtures. Avoid wiping the bulbs and make sure they are cool and turned off before you begin.

Part II: Bedroom Checklists

DAILY BEDROOM CHECKLIST

	TASKS
☐	Pick up any toys, clothes, trash, or other items that have made their way to the floor during the day.
☐	Straighten items on shelves and put away anything that doesn't belong there.
☐	Make the bed and straighten the pillows.
☐	Open and close blinds and curtains as appropriate.
☐	Straighten the top of the dresser and nightstands and put away any clutter.
☐	Place all dirty clothes in a hamper.

WEEKLY BEDROOM CHECKLIST

	TASKS
☐	Vacuum or mop the floor, as appropriate.
☐	Shake out area rugs.
☐	Wipe down all baseboards.
☐	Clean up any scuffmarks.
☐	Dust shelves, top and bottom.
☐	Dust the bedframe.
☐	Put away any items that have accumulated under the bed.
☐	Change the linens.
☐	Wipe down windows and blinds.
☐	Wipe out the window tracks.
☐	Wipe down the dresser.
☐	Organize dresser drawers.
☐	Do the laundry. *Note:* Don't forget to grab the cleaning rags, dishrags, bathroom towels, and

	linens when you start the laundry for the week.
☐	Put away laundry as soon as possible, to reduce both wrinkles and the likelihood that it will be forgotten or avoided.
☐	Dust all light fixtures.

MONTHLY BEDROOM CHECKLIST

	TASKS
☐	Wash rugs.
☐	Wipe out shelves with all-purpose cleaner.
☐	Wipe down the bedframe with all-purpose cleaner.
☐	Wash the blankets.
☐	Wash the inside window panes.
☐	Wash the outside window panes quarterly.
☐	Pick up and put away anything that has fallen behind or under the dresser, bookshelves, end tables, and bed in preparation for vacuuming/mopping.
☐	Wipe down all light fixtures. Avoid wiping the bulbs and make sure they are cool and turned off before you begin.

8. Cleaning the Family Room

Part I: Cleaning Tips and Strategies for the Family Room

Floors

Daily:

- Walk through and put away anything that has been left out, such as clothes, toys, or books. Throw out any trash.

Weekly:

- Vacuum or sweep and mop as appropriate.
- Wipe down baseboards.

- Remove scuffmarks.

Monthly:

- Wash or beat area rugs.

Walls

Daily:

- Wipe up any splatters on the walls.

Weekly:

- Wipe down walls with all-purpose cleaner.
- Wipe down baseboards.
- Clean off scuff marks.
- Wipe off outlet covers and light switches.

Monthly:

- Wash the walls with a mild solution of soap and water (3-4 drops of liquid castile soap to 1 gallon of warm water) or mix vinegar and warm water (2-3 Tablespoons of distilled white vinegar to 1 gallon of warm water). Don't soak the walls – instead, wet a soft sponge in the cleaning solution, wring it out, and gently wash the walls. Make sure that the sponge is nearly dry before washing around outlets and light switches. Disconnect power to outlets for an added safety measure.

Entertainment Center

Daily:

- Straighten movies, books, magazines, and electronics.

Weekly:

- Dust the entertainment center. Don't forget behind the television and the electronics cords. A vacuum hose with a narrow attachment can work great for getting at dust that has gathered around cords. Just be careful not to suck any cords into the vacuum.

Monthly:

- Wipe down the entertainment center.
- Clean any glass components, including cupboard fronts and shelves.
- Declutter books and magazines.

Tables

Daily:

- Straighten magazines and put away anything that has been left out on a table

Weekly:

- Wipe down the coffee table and any other high-use tables such as catch-alls and end tables.

Monthly:

- Wipe out any drawers and cupboards built into your tables.

Bookshelves

Daily:

- Straighten books and other items.

Weekly:

- Dust the bookshelves, including the books themselves and the tops of shelving units.

Monthly:

- None.

Light Fixtures

Daily:

- No daily tasks.

Weekly:

- Dust all light fixtures.

Monthly:

- Wipe down all light fixtures. Avoid wiping the bulbs and make sure they are cool and turned off before you begin.

Windows/Window Treatments

Daily:

- Open and close curtains/blinds at the appropriate times of day.

Weekly:

- Wipe down blinds.
- Wipe down windows.

- Dust off the tops of all window treatments.

Monthly:

- No monthly tasks.

Upholstered Furniture

Daily:

- Straighten cushions.
- Fold throws.

Weekly:

- Clean out items that may have fallen between or under seat cushions.
- Vacuum the furniture.

Monthly:

- Clean under and behind furniture in preparation for vacuuming the floor.

Part II: Family Room Checklists

DAILY FAMILY ROOM CHECKLIST

	TASKS
☐	Walk through and put away anything that has been left out, such as clothes, toys, or books. Throw out any trash.
☐	Wipe up any splatters on the walls.
☐	Straighten movies, books, magazines, and electronics in the entertainment center.
☐	Straighten magazines and put away anything that has been left out on a table.
☐	Straighten books and other items on bookshelves.
☐	Open and close curtains/blinds at the appropriate times of day.
☐	Straighten cushions.
☐	Fold throws.

WEEKLY FAMILY ROOM CHECKLIST

	TASKS
☐	Vacuum or sweep and mop as appropriate.
☐	Wipe down baseboards.
☐	Remove scuffmarks.
☐	Wipe down walls.
☐	Wipe off outlet covers and light switches.
☐	Dust the entertainment center.
☐	Wipe down the coffee table and any other high-use tables such as catch-alls and end tables.
☐	Dust the bookshelves, including the books themselves and the tops of shelving units.
☐	Dust all light fixtures.
☐	Wipe down blinds.
☐	Wipe down windows.
☐	Dust off the tops of all window treatments.
☐	Clean out items that may have fallen between or

	under seat cushions.
☐	Vacuum the furniture.

MONTHLY FAMILY ROOM CHECKLIST

	TASKS
☐	Wash or beat area rugs.
☐	Wash walls.
☐	Wipe down the entertainment center.
☐	Clean any glass components.
☐	Declutter books and magazines.
☐	Wipe out any drawers and cupboards built into your tables.
☐	Wipe down all light fixtures. Avoid wiping the bulbs and make sure they are cool and turned off.
☐	Clean under and behind furniture in preparation for vacuuming the floor.

9. Cleaning the Hallways

Part I: Cleaning Tips and Strategies for the Hallways

Walls

Daily:

- No daily tasks

Weekly:

- Wipe down the walls.
- Wipe down the baseboards.
- Clean any scuffmarks from walls and baseboards.

Monthly:

- Wash the walls with a mild solution of soap and water (3-4 drops of liquid castile soap to 1 gallon of warm water) or mix vinegar and warm water (2-3 Tablespoons of distilled white vinegar to 1 gallon of warm water). Don't soak the walls – instead, wet a soft sponge in the cleaning solution, wring it out, and gently wash the walls. Make sure that the sponge is nearly dry before washing around outlets and light switches. Disconnect power to outlets for an added safety measure.

Floors

Daily:

- Walk through and pick up anything that has been left in the hallway (i.e., shoes, bags).

Weekly:

- Sweep and mop or vacuum, as appropriate.
- Shake out or vacuum any rugs.
- Wipe down baseboards
- Remove scuffmarks

Monthly:

- Wash any rugs.

Stairs

Daily:

- Pick up clutter and other items that may have made their way to the stairs.

Weekly:

- Sweep and mop or vacuum, as appropriate.
- Dust banisters.

Monthly:

- Wipe down banisters, including the floor area between rails.

Pictures and Wall Hangings

Daily:

- No daily tasks.

Weekly:

- Dust picture frames and wall hangings.

Monthly:

- Wipe down picture frames.

Furniture

Daily:

- If you have side tables or other furniture in your hallway, put away anything on them that doesn't belong.

Weekly:

- Dust the furniture.

Monthly:

- Wipe down the surfaces of hallway furniture with all-purpose cleaner. Consider adding a few drops of lemon or orange essential oil for a more pleasant smell and shine on wood furniture.

Part II: Hallway Checklists

DAILY HALLWAY CHECKLIST

	TASKS
☐	Walk through and pick up anything that has been left in the hallway (i.e., shoes, bags).
☐	Pick up clutter and other items that may have made their way to the stairs.
☐	If you have side tables or other furniture in your hallway, put away anything on them that doesn't belong.

WEEKLY HALLWAY CHECKLIST

	TABLE
☐	Wipe down the walls.
☐	Wipe down the baseboards.

□	Clean any scuffmarks from walls and baseboards.
□	Sweep and mop or vacuum, as appropriate.
□	Shake out or vacuum any rugs.
□	Sweep and mop or vacuum the stairs, as appropriate.
□	Dust banisters.
□	Dust picture frames and wall hangings.
□	Dust the furniture.

MONTHLY HALLWAY CHECKLIST

	TABLE
□	Wash the walls.
□	Wash any rugs.
□	Wipe down banisters, including the floor area between rails.
□	Wipe down picture frames.
□	Wipe down the surfaces of hallway furniture.

10.   Cleaning the Closets

Part I: Cleaning Tips and Strategies for the Closets

Daily:

- Straighten shelves, floors, and hanging racks.

Weekly:

- Wipe down closet doors, door handles, and visible surface of shelves.

Monthly:

- Vacuum or sweep the closet floor.
- Organize shelves and get rid of clutter.
- Remove scuffmarks.
- Declutter and organize contents.
- Wash the shelves.

Part II: Closet Checklists

DAILY/WEEKLY/MONTHLY CLOSET CHECKLIST

	DAILY TASKS
☐	Straighten shelves, floors, and hanging racks.
	WEEKLY TASKS
☐	Wipe down closet doors, door handles, and visible surface of shelves.
	MONTHLY TASKS
☐	Vacuum or sweep the closet floor.
☐	Organize shelves and get rid of clutter.
☐	Remove scuffmarks.
☐	Declutter and organize contents.
☐	Wash the shelves.

11. Green Cleaning

In this chapter you will find the basic green cleaning recipes referred to throughout this book. These recipes are simple to prepare, cost effective, and in most cases, multipurpose. Cleaning green doesn't have to be complicated or cost an arm and a leg. The key is knowing which ingredients to use in your homemade green cleaning products, including knowing which ingredients are best suited for which cleaning purposes. Let's take a look at some of the common green cleaning ingredients included in the formulations and cleaning strategies given in this book.

Vinegar. Although vinegar is often touted as a cure-all for cheap, effective, natural cleaning, the truth is that vinegar is not suited to every purpose. For example, it can be great as a natural disinfectant, but is not always so helpful when it comes to scrubbing dirt and grime off of surfaces. Vinegar is most useful as a natural disinfectant, for removal of mineral, soap scum, and oil buildup, and as a tarnish remover, deodorizer, and drain cleaner.

Castile Soap. Castile soap is made from vegetable oils (such as coconut, olive, and avocado oils) as opposed to animal fats. It comes in bar and liquid forms and can be used to clean everything from countertops to toilets to laundry detergent. For maximum effectiveness, avoid mixing Castile soap with vinegar, hydrogen peroxide, or other acids and avoid using with hard water, as these combinations reduce the effectiveness of the soap and can cause it to leave behind a white film.

Hydrogen Peroxide. Hydrogen peroxide can be used as a natural disinfectant and also has bleaching properties. It is considered safe for household use and is a very useful ingredient in many green cleaning solutions. Hydrogen peroxide should be kept in an opaque spray-bottle as it loses its effectiveness as a disinfectant when exposed to light. Note that any cleaning solution which uses hydrogen peroxide should be color tested on an inconspicuous part of the surface to be cleaned prior to actual cleaning.

Baking Soda. Sodium bicarbonate, or baking soda, comes naturally from nahcolite mined from the Earth or through a chemical reaction process from trona ore, also mined from the Earth. Baking soda is useful as a disinfectant, stain remover, mild cleaning abrasive, and deodorizer.

Essential Oils. Essential oils are natural oils obtained through the distillation of various plant species. They can serve a variety of purposes depending on the oil type, including as disinfectants, degreasers, and deodorizers. Although essential oils can be a little more expensive than other items mentioned in this chapter, you usually only need a few drops in a single recipe, so they go a long way.

These 5 ingredients form the basis of many green cleaning recipes and strategies that can be implemented throughout the home. However, keep in mind that these are not the only natural cleaning ingredients out there. Other ingredients, such as borax, have not been including in this chapter because they aren't used in any of the cleaning recipes or strategies in the book. I prefer these five basic ingredients because they are relatively inexpensive, natural, safe, and usually quite easy to use.

Do-It-Yourself Green Cleaners

1. Wood Floor Cleaner

Ingredients:

- 1.5 cups hot water
- 1½ tsp borax
- ½ tsp lemon or orange oil
- ½ Tbsp liquid dish soap (not castile)
- ¼ cup white vinegar

Mix ingredients and add to a spray bottle. Spray down wooden floors and mop up with a damp mop.

2. Grout Cleaner

Ingredients:

- Hydrogen peroxide
- Baking soda

Mix 1 part hydrogen peroxide with 3 parts baking soda in a bowl. Scrub the paste into the grout. Let sit for 30 minutes, then wipe away the paste and rinse. *color test in an inconspicuous area before use.

3. All-Purpose Cleaner, Vinegar Based

Ingredients:

- Distilled white vinegar
- Water
- Essential oil of your choice (recommended: peppermint)

Mix equal parts vinegar and water in a spray bottle. Add 12 drops of essential oil. Shake well. Spray on the intended surface and wipe or scrub with a damp rag.

4. All-Purpose Cleaner, Hydrogen Peroxide Based

Ingredients:

- Hydrogen peroxide
- Water

Mix 1 part hydrogen peroxide with 1 part water in an opaque spray bottle. Spray on the intended surface and wipe or scrub with a damp rag.

5. *Countertop Stain-Remover and Disinfectant*

Ingredients:

- Hydrogen peroxide
- Baking soda

Mix 1 Tbsp baking soda with 2 Tbsp hydrogen peroxide. Scrub paste into countertop stains. Let sit for 30 minutes. Wipe up with a damp rag.

6. *Natural Degreaser*

Ingredients:

- 1 cup distilled white vinegar
- 1 cup warm water
- 1 Tbsp baking soda
- 3 drops liquid dish soap (not castile)
- 5 drops lemon or orange essential oil

Mix all ingredients in a spray bottle. Shake vigorously. Apply to area in need of degreasing. Let sit for 5-10 minutes, then wipe clean with a damp rag or sponge.

7. *Glass Cleaner*

Ingredients:

- 1 cup water
- ¾ cup rubbing alcohol
- 2 Tbsp white distilled vinegar

Mix all ingredients in a spray bottle. Store away from heat sources as this mixture is flammable.

8. Castile Liquid Laundry Detergent

Ingredients:

- ¼ cup Epsom salt
- ½ cup washing soda
- ¼ cup baking soda
- 1 cup liquid castile soap
- 1 gallon water

Boil 4 cups of water in a large pot. Dissolve salt, washing soda, and baking soda into the water. Allow to cool until lukewarm. Pour into a sealable container, add the remaining water and castile soap. Stir before use. Use ½ - ¾ cup for a normal load of laundry.

Printed in Great Britain
by Amazon